Percy Kidner in an early Vauxhall single-cylinder in 1904/5. Kidner (1878-1969) joined Vauxhall in 1904, was engineering director from 1907 but had left by 1928, becoming an Aston Martin director. In his old age he regularly drove a works-owned Vauxhall like this one in the Brighton Run and built magnificent model locomotives and ships, leaving the contents of his workshop on his death to his old school, Blundells, at Tiverton in Devon.

THE VAUXHALL

Peter Hull

Shire Publications Ltd

CONTENTS

Printed in Great Britain by C. I. Thomas & Sons (Haverfordwest) Ltd, Press Buildings, Merlins Bridge, Haverfordwest, Dyfed SA61 1XF.

British Library Cataloguing in Publication Data: Hull, Peter. Vauxhall. — (Shire Albums Series; No. 288). I. Title. II. Series. 629.222. ISBN 0-7478-0183-5.

Editorial Consultant: Michael E. Ware, Curator of the National Motor Museum, Beaulieu.

ACKNOWLEDGEMENTS
The author is grateful to Nic Portway for the cover photograph of his car and to the National Motor Museum for supplying all the other photographs from the Vauxhall Motors collection at Beaulieu, of which some of the early ones are from Percy Kidner's personal albums.

Cover: *This 1922 E-type 30-98 has belonged to Nic Portway since 1963. 30-98s excelled in hill climbs and sprints and broke long-distance town to town records in Australia and South Africa. Some 30-98s had saloon bodies. The fastest 30-98 Brooklands lap was by an OE Velox four-seater at 114.23 mph (184 km/h) in 1932.*

Below: *A 1905 18 hp, designed by F. W. Hodges and built at Luton, and the first four-cylinder Vauxhall. Shaft drive was standardised, but some cars had chains, and the famous Vauxhall bonnet flutes are in evidence for the first time.*

A 1905 four-seater 2.4 litre three-cylinder 12/14 hp with three separate vertical cylinders.

BEGINNINGS AND EARLY YEARS, 1903-7

The beginnings of what became Vauxhall Motors can be traced to the Wandsworth Road, London SW8, where in 1857 a firm named Alexander Wilson and Company was founded to manufacture in the old Vauxhall Ironworks premises steam engines to be used in Admiralty pinnaces, river tugs and Thames pleasure paddle boats, and also pumps and refrigeration plant. In 1892 a limited company was formed but Wilson resigned from it to set himself up as a consultant engineer. A receiver was appointed in 1896, and in 1897 Wilson's name was dropped and the firm was retitled 'The Vauxhall Ironworks Company Limited', with some 150 employees. Vauxhall, a district just south of the Thames, was famous for its pleasure gardens, opened in 1661. After a grand gala the gardens closed in 1859, just two years after Wilson had set up his company.

The man who must be credited with the birth of the Vauxhall car is F. W. Hodges, who had served his apprenticeship with Alexander Wilson and Company as a marine engineer. Hodges got the company to buy a car (probably a Canstatt-Daimler) in order to study it with a view to eventual car production. Two experimental belt-driven cars were made, but it was not until 1902 that Hodges and J. H. Chambers (who had been called in as a receiver in 1896 and then joined the board) began work on the design of what was to become the first Vauxhall production car.

This new model, a £136 light two-seater runabout, made its appearance in 1903, with a 989 cc horizontal single-cylinder engine with automatic inlet valve, tiller steering, single chain drive and a two-speed epicyclic gearbox with no reverse. It was governed down to 18 mph (30 km/h), but when a

3

pedal was pressed to override the governor 25 mph (40 km/h) was possible in high gear. The engine produced its 5 brake horsepower (bhp) at 900 revolutions per minute (rpm) and 43 cars were produced.

In February 1904 a more powerful £150 1039 cc version was brought out with a reverse gear. It successfully proved it was no town runabout when a Vauxhall director, Percy C. Kidner, drove it in the Glasgow to London Trial on the 19th/20th May 1905. It was the smallest car entered but he lost only seven marks out of one thousand, denoting seven minutes to change a plug, and he never had to come to an involuntary halt on a hill as did several of his rivals in larger-capacity cars. In September 1904 a steering wheel replaced the tiller on this 6 hp model, and in November Hodges produced an entirely new model, the 12/14 horsepower, costing £375.

This 2.4 litre car had three separately cast vertical cylinders in an engine with two camshafts and side-valves in a T-head, a three-speed gearbox, double chain drive and half-elliptic leaf springs all round instead of small coil springs as on the single-cylinder cars. Later a smaller 1.3 litre 7/9 hp model was produced and an enlarged 1.4 litre 9 hp. These three-cylinder cars had the same pointed prow above an oblong radiator matrix like previous single-cylinder models but were bigger and could have four-seater bodies.

Meanwhile there were problems over the lease of the London factory, and over lack of space there, where completed cars had to be brought out of the basement by a hoist — the telegraphic address was 'Wellhole, London'. Thus a move was made early in 1905 to a 7 acre (2.8 hectare) site on the outskirts of Luton, 30 miles (48 km) north of London, where the Vauxhall Ironworks amalgamated with a neighbouring firm, the West Hydraulic Engineering Company Limited to form Vauxhall and West Hydraulic, the former continuing its car and marine work.

Those 7 acres eventually had to grow to some 300 acres (121 hectares) to contain the Vauxhall works.

A special 12/14 three-cylinder car was entered for the first Isle of Man Tourist Trophy (TT) race in 1905 fitted with a six-speed gearbox. Alfred John Hancock, known as 'AJ' or 'Joey', a former Vauxhall marine-engine apprentice, was the driver, but on the second lap he broke a wheel and retired.

In the same year Hodges produced the first four-cylinder Vauxhall, the 18 hp, with a 3402 cc T-head engine with five main bearings, first with chain drive and then with shaft drive, with a four-speed gearbox and costing £475. This was the first Vauxhall with cutaway flutes down each side of the bonnet from the radiator rearwards, a trademark for the next fifty years.

The merger with West Hydraulic was not a success and in 1907 the car side of the business was sold off for £17,000 to a young director, Leslie Walton, who became chairman, and his co-director, Percy Kidner, responsible for the engineering side. Later they took over the West Hydraulic premises. In 1906 a brilliant young engineer, 23-year-old Laurence Pomeroy, joined as assistant to Hodges and in 1907 produced his first Vauxhall design, to replace the 18 hp. It had a similar T-head four-cylinder engine with five main bearings but of 2.5 rather than 3.4 litres, of nearly square dimensions, 92 by 95 mm, producing 23.5 bhp at 1800 rpm to the 18 bhp at 950 rpm of its predecessor. It had a three-speed gearbox, shaft drive and at £375 sold better than the 18 hp. Although the Pomeroy design had a 20.25 hp RAC rating it was given the uninformative title of 12/16 hp, presumably as a follow-on from the three-cylinder 12/14, which had been discontinued after 1905, whereas the 18 hp continued to be sold alongside the new 12/16 until the end of 1907.

One of the first pointed-radiator Prince Henry cars outside the Lyn Valley Hotel at Lynmouth, Devon, at Easter 1911, with Laurence Pomeroy at the wheel. These cars were severely tested on the Devon hills, and this travel-stained example seems already to have had part of its front number plate knocked away.

THE SPORTING VAUXHALLS, 1908-27

The RAC 2000 Miles (3219 km) International Touring Car Trial of 1908, a fifteen-day event over English and Scottish roads, starting in London, with Inverness as the furthest point north, and finishing with a speed test on Brooklands track, Surrey, brought the first real fame to the Vauxhall name. Vauxhall entered one car, described as a 12/16 hp, to be driven by Percy Kidner, who covered the distance without any adjustment, repair or replacement, had no punctures or tyre stops and did not even have to add water or oil. With a clean score sheet, the Vauxhall won its class and scored best marks overall. Though entered as a 12/16 hp, this paragon was a new model designed by Pomeroy as soon as the Trial regulations were published. The four-cylinder engine had the more efficient L-head side-valve arrangement, replacing the T-head of the previous models, and a White & Poppe carburettor and an accelerator pedal instead of the lever on the steering wheel operating wedges to accelerate the engine by giving more lift to the inlet valves. This five-main-bearing, 91 by 120.65 mm, 3138 cc engine gave 39 bhp at 2370 rpm and is important as it was the basis of all sporting Vauxhall engines up to the mid 1920s.

For 1909 the original 12/16 hp model was continued for its final year, but two new models were introduced: the A-type 20 hp four-cylinder production version of the 2000 Miles Trial winner with the monobloc engine slightly reduced to 90 by 120 mm, 3053 cc, and a more robust chassis, called the 16/20 hp; and a smaller B-type version, the 16 hp, with an 85 by 102 mm, 2315 cc engine. The 16 hp had three speeds, the 16/20 four.

20 hp cars had class wins in the Irish and Scottish road trials and in stripped chassis form won six races at Brooklands with Kidner, Hancock and a Vauxhall director, Rudolf Selz, as the drivers. At the end of

Above: *The famous 20 hp 3.1 litre four-cylinder car with a monobloc engine designed by the young Laurence Pomeroy, who took over from F. W. Hodges, seen here on its way to winning the 1908 RAC 2000 Miles Trial. Kidner is at the wheel, ex-apprentice A. J. Hancock by his side, and an RAC observer is in the back.*

Below: *A. J. Hancock at the wheel of the first Vauxhall single-seater racing car, KN, with 20 hp engine, at Brooklands in 1909. Note the enormously long starting handle clipped to the side of the chassis.*

the season Hancock took 21 hp class sprint records at Brooklands with a single-seater 20 hp developing 52.6 bhp, known as KN ('hot as Cayenne pepper'), which pioneered the slim wind-resisting racing car with bodywork scarcely wider than Hancock's shoulders.

For 1910 the first six-cylinder Vauxhall was announced with two blocks of three cylinders, 90 by 120 mm, like a '20' with two extra cylinders, giving 4580 cc and 29.6 bhp; it was known as the '30', a luxury model. In this year three '20' 3.1 litre 60 bhp 72 mph (116 km/h) cars were prepared for the Prince Henry Trial in Prussia, with light doorless four-seater bodies and unusual pointed fluted radiators driven by Kidner and Hancock, who incurred no penalties, and Selz, who received minor penalties. Victory on formula went to the 5.7 litre Austro-Daimler of its designer driver, Dr Porsche. Successes continued in hill climbs and sprints, and at Brooklands A. J. Hancock was the first man to achieve 100 mph (160.43 km/h) in a 20 hp car, driving a new single-seater Vauxhall fitted with KN's engine over the flying half-mile (0.8 km).

By 1911 the '16' had been dropped and only a short- or long-chassis A-type '20' and the B-type six cylinder '30' were offered, but during the year the new sporting

A. J. Hancock in the driving seat of the 3 litre racing Prince Henry he drove in the 1911 Coupe des Voitures Légères race at Boulogne. He retired on his third lap after breaking a connecting rod. This was Vauxhall's first continental race.

55 bhp C-type 20 hp 'Prince Henry' model was on sale with pointed fluted radiator and a replica Prince Henry Trial doorless body as an option. At Brooklands Hancock took short-distance records in the 16 hp (80 mm bore) class at speeds up to 91.64 mph (147.18 km/h) in a single-seater with a special tall engine with an outsize stroke of 200 mm (7.8 inches) which stuck out through the top of the bonnet. He failed

Kidner's Prince Henry, with high ground clearance and no bonnet flutes, between a T-model Ford on the left and a Benz on the right during the 1911 Russian Trial, from St Petersburg to Sebastopol. Because there were no hotels, a train ran parallel to the route, and competitors slept in the train during the overnight stops.

A 35 hp six-cylinder car exhibited at the 1912 London Olympia Show, with the flat Vauxhall radiator of the period. The bodywork was favoured by the Russian imperial family and nobility, allowing entry to the rear by passengers wearing formal headgear. It incorporated a bodyguard's seat on the running board which could be folded and stored in the cavity in the scuttle protected by a detachable panel.

Kidner drove this Prince Henry in the 1912 Swedish Trial, held in deep snow, from Stockholm to Gothenburg and back.

with a broken connecting rod in a two-seater racing-bodied Prince Henry with a slightly reduced stroke 3 litre engine in the Coupe des Voitures Légères race at Boulogne, but Kidner won his class in a Prince Henry in the 1400 mile (2250 km) Russian Trial from St Petersburg to Sebastopol, which led to a flourishing export trade to Russia and a Vauxhall depot in St Petersburg.

In 1912 the flat radiator 20 hp had a chassis price of £440, the Prince Henry £485 and the six-cylinder 30 hp £600. In February Kidner drove a Prince Henry in freezing conditions in the Swedish Trial, but it was the Swedish agent Hjalmar Kjellgren in a flat radiator '20' who came second to the Winter Cup winner's 40 hp Opel. There were three single-seater wins at Brooklands, Hancock and Percy Lambert driving. Hancock, Lambert and the Liverpool Vauxhall agent, Willie Watson, retired in the 3 litre Coupe de l'Auto part of the French Grand Prix at Dieppe, but Hancock took the 50 mile 21 hp class world record at 97.15 mph (156.34 km/h) in a single-seater with a 3 litre Coupe de l'Auto engine.

At this time Harry Varley, a Vauxhall apprentice, later associated with the 3 litre Bentley design, won a competition to design a new Vauxhall badge; he revived the griffin (part lion, part eagle) emblem of Wilson's firm and of Vauxhall Gardens. The name 'Vauxhall' is a contraction of 'Fulke's Hall', the hall having been built by Fulke le Breant, a thirteenth-century soldier, whose emblem was the griffin and who, strangely, also owned land at Luton.

In 1913 the 3.1 litre A-type was supplemented by the B-type six-cylinder with a bore increase to 95 mm, producing 5 litres and a 33 hp RAC rating, although it was known as the 35 hp, and a similar bore increase gave the C-type Prince Henry 95 by 140 mm and 3969 cc, as it did the new D-type with the 4 litre engine detuned and a longer wheelbase.

1913 was a momentous year in which a C-type Prince Henry engine enlarged to 98 by 150 mm, 4.5 litres, was put into a short-wheelbase Prince Henry chassis with a light four-seater body and flat radiator for Joseph

Willie Watson and his mechanic, Vauxhall engineer Jock Payne, in the 1913 Coupe de l'Auto race at Boulogne in a Prince Henry based 3 litre '20', now with the new flat radiator, instead of the pointed one of the previous year, and the unusual nautical-type alloy steering wheel. Watson went out on the last lap with a broken back axle, but his team mate, Hancock, finished in fourth place.

Higginson, a leading hill-climber. The car was known as the 30-98, one theory being it filled the vacant slot between the 25 hp C- and D-types and the 35 hp B-type six, and the addition of the 98 for the bore made a euphonious model name. Higginson made the fastest time at Waddington Fells hill climb and broke the record at Shelsley Walsh, whilst Hancock broke the Aston Hill record with a 30-98 powered Coupe de l'Auto racer and lapped Brooklands at 108.03 mph (173.85 km/h) in a 30-98 engined single-seater. Then in September Hancock came fourth in the 388 mile (624 km) Coupe de l'Auto race at Boulogne in a two-seater 3 litre '20' behind two twin-cam sixteen-valve Peugeots and Lee Guinness's side-valve four-cylinder Sunbeam. At Brooklands Hancock in a new 4 litre single-

A 1914 E-type 30-98, originally the property of Percy Kidner, with unusual cantilever rear springing. This must be a wartime photograph, to judge by the masks on the sidelights, which could be hinged forward, when not in use, by remote control from the driver's seat.

seater Prince Henry, 'KN2', abandoned his twelve-hour record attempt when a front spring shackle broke after 9½ hours, but he collected two class and six world records up to 9 hours at 83.31 mph (134 km/h) from up to 2 hours at 92.72 mph (149 km/h).

The 30-98 sold in 1914 at £900 for the chassis compared with £515 for the Prince Henry. A team of advanced Pomeroy-designed twin-cam four-cylinder sixteen-valve engined cars in 3 litre form for the Isle of Man TT and 4½ litre form for the French

The distinguished American driver Ralph de Palma in the 4½ litre version of the TT cars at the French Grand Prix at Lyons in 1914. His car, and those of Hancock and Watson, did not get beyond the seventh lap because of fuel starvation, air pressure in the fuel tanks having been inadvisedly reduced.

10

A. J. Hancock in his 1914 twin-cam 3 litre TT car taking Hillberry corner in the Isle of Man. Vauxhall had a dreadful race: the cars of Watson and Higginson went out on the first lap with engine trouble, whilst Hancock and his mechanic, Gibbs, struggled on until the second day, when their car crashed and turned over on the Mountain.

King George V, seated behind the driver, reviews a battalion of the Scots Guards during the First World War from a standard War Office model 25 hp D-type Vauxhall staff car. This was developed into the postwar overhead-valve OD 23/60 hp fitted with the impressively named 'Lanchester Harmonic Balancer' to neutralise crankshaft vibration.

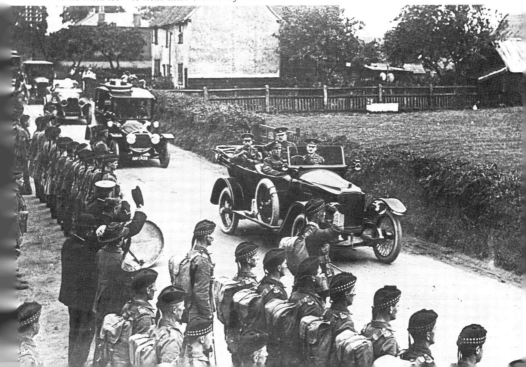

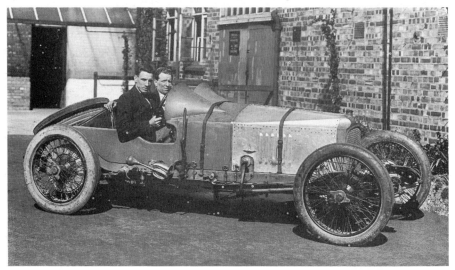

Matthew Park, repair shop foreman, at the wheel of his 3 litre, sixteen-valve 1922 TT Vauxhall, which had two detachable bronze heads, one to each pair of cylinders, and Perrot-type front brake actuation. Park and Ernest Swain, road test department foreman, retired in the TT, but Jock Payne, finished vehicles foreman, in the third car, gained third place.

This is a 1922 TT Vauxhall in unlikely 1930/1 Vauxhall Villiers Supercharge form with strengthened chassis and new square radiator — a successful sprint car, heavier, but much more powerful. What looks like a machine gun is the external supercharger intercooler, and behind are the car's constructors, Raymond Mays (driver), Peter Berthon (centre) and Amherst Villiers, with his hand on Mays's 3 litre Lagonda saloon.

The disc-wheeled M-type 14 hp Vauxhall had cantilever rear springs and made extensive use of light alloy in the cylinder head, pistons, connecting rods (duralumin), sump, gearbox casing, torque tube and back axle housing. Its successor, the wire-wheeled 1925 LM 14/40 hp, was a bigger, faster car, examples of which were experimentally fitted with Wilson preselector gearboxes.

Grand Prix at Lyons all failed, though redeeming themselves by their Brooklands performances during the 1921 season.

During the First World War Vauxhall made millions of detonator caps for shells, but their famous wartime product was the 25 hp D-type staff car, of which nearly two thousand were made. In 1919 Pomeroy left Vauxhall and Clarence E. King took his place. For 1920 the D-type cost £1450 complete and the E-type 30-98 £1675, now with aluminium pistons and electric lighting. With around 85 mph (137 km/h) maximum speed in standard trim, it was one of the fastest production cars in the world. One of three very advanced racing 3 litre twin-cam sixteen-valve Vauxhalls, with engines designed by H. R. Ricardo and four-wheel-braked chassis by C. E. King, came third in the 1922 Tourist Trophy behind a GP Sunbeam and a 3 litre Bentley, and one of these cars lapped Brooklands at

112.42 mph (181 km/h) in 1926, another becoming the Vauxhall Villiers Special.

Also in 1922 came King's updated 4.2 litre OE type 30-98 with a reduced-stroke 98 by 140 mm engine, duralumin connecting rods, and overhead valves, with duralumin pushrods, in a detachable head. The D-type with similar valve gear became the OD 23/60 hp. Completely new was King's £595 side-valve 14 hp 2.3 litre four-cylinder M-type with detachable Ricardo alloy head and three-speed gearbox integral with the engine. In 1923 the OE and OD were both given front-wheel brakes and in 1925 the M-type became the LM 14/40 hp with four speeds and four-wheel brakes and 65 mph (105 km/h), the last side-valve Vauxhall to be made.

In 1925 Vauxhall Motors was bought by General Motors (GM) of America, giving them their first foothold in Europe.

Vauxhall Motors' own 1926 OE 30-98 Velox tourer, photographed in the 1950s. There are four-wheel brakes and E-type beaded-edge wheels have been replaced by split (not wellbase) rims with straight-sided tyres. Now with 120 bhp instead of 90 bhp, a balanced crank gave more refinement, but there was less torque and a heavier chassis. Competition successes continued into the 1930s.

The 1928-31 20/60 hp R- and T-type General Motors Vauxhalls of 2.7, 2.9 and 3.3 litres, initially with artillery wheels, were moderately priced, roomy, low-geared family cars with good brakes. Here is a 3.3 litre 1930 T80 75 mph (120 km/h) Hurlingham sports-bodied roadster.

Balloon tyres on wellbase rims and a tubular front axle featured on the sleeve-valve luxury 25/70 3.9 litre S-type, 1925-8. The 2 tonne kerb weight rather inhibited the 25/70's lively engine.

GENERAL MOTORS FAMILY CARS, 1928-56

Initially Vauxhall carried on much as before the takeover, the 30-98 continuing until 1927, by which time it had been given larger brake drums and hydraulic front and transmission brakes, the technology of the leather seals of the time causing fluid leaks and unreliability. The last design of the old regime, with similar braking, was the new six-cylinder S-type 25/70 hp, which had a Ricardo engine with single-sleeve valves designed under Burt McCollum patents of 3.9 litres with a crankshaft with ten main bearings. As on the 1922 TT cars, the flywheel was centrally mounted on the crankshaft. It was a heavy and expensive luxury car, costing up to £1675; few were made and production ceased after three years in 1928.

From 1928 to 1931 there was a one-model policy based on the new £495 2762 cc seven-main-bearing six-cylinder pushrod R-type 20/60 hp with a four-speed box. Though designed at Luton, it was an amalgam of Luton and Detroit features, in which the more cost-effective items (Delco-Remy coil ignition, Borg and Beck clutch, Oakland-type rear axle, pressed-steel instead of alloy castings, cast-iron pistons,

artillery wheels and so on) showed American influence, whilst the admittedly effective brakes (but reportedly with 132 parts between brake cable and shoe), complicated internal oil pressure circulation and complex engineering of the king-pins (needing fourteen different lathe operations) were probably Luton contributions. C. E. King was held responsible for overall design, an obligation he was to carry out at Vauxhall until his retirement in 1954. The work of various coachbuilders augmented the standard bodywork.

From 1929 the bore was enlarged from 73 to 75 mm, giving 2915 cc with the 110 mm stroke. Aluminium pistons were fitted, as was an American-type ball central gear change. Then in 1930 came the T-type, with an 80 mm bore giving 3317 cc, also known as the Silent 80, because it had a direct-drive silent third gear. It featured a stiffer chassis and Luvax hydraulic shock absorbers and did over 70 mph (112.6 km/h).

The breakthrough came with the £280 VY Cadet at the 1930 Motor Show, a value-for-money family saloon with no legacy from its sporting and luxury antecedents. This had a 2045 cc six-cylinder pushrod engine, rubber-mounted, with a four-bearing pressure-fed crankshaft and a three-speed gearbox, augmented in 1932 with synchromesh on second and top gears, the first British car so fitted and just ahead of Rolls-Royce. There were 6 volt electrics and a suction-operated windscreen wiper, also modified American Bendix brakes. Meanwhile Bedford commercial vehicles began production at Luton in 1931 and their better sales supported the cars, the VX Cadet for export having a 3.2 litre Bedford engine. The VY Cadet had a maximum speed of 62.07 mph (100 km/h).

The first big-selling Vauxhall was the AS series Light Six, the £195 12 hp rated ASY version of 1933 having a 1531 cc engine with a four-speed synchromesh gearbox, 12 volts and an electric wiper. It was joined in 1934 by the slightly larger £225 ASX 14 hp with a 1782 cc engine and twin wipers. Also in 1934 there were two BY and BX Big Sixes, costing over £300, of 2.4 and 3.2 litres, the latter bigger-bore car capable of just over 70 mph (112 km/h) like the 14 hp ASX.

For 1935 the new DY and DX 12 and 14 hp Light Sixes had a simplified version of Dubonnet independent front suspension (ifs) built under licence by General Motors from the original design of the Frenchman Gustave Chedru, who was financed by the former racing driver André Dubonnet, of the drinks firm. GM used Dubonnet suspension on Chevrolet and Pontiac cars in the USA and on Vauxhall and Opel in Europe, the latter German firm having been taken over by GM in 1929. Cadillac, Buick and Oldsmobile, the other American GM makes, used more conventional coil and wishbone systems.

For 1937 the Big Sixes were replaced by the competitively priced £298 four-speed GY '25', capable of over 81 mph (130 km/h), also Dubonnet equipped, called GL in long-chassis form. Restyled DX and DY

This is a 1932 2 litre Cadet, which replaced the bigger and more expensive 20/60s. Its British-style leather trim, sliding roof and pressure lubrication disassociated it from GM's splash-lubricated Chevrolets. It was the first British car with synchromesh.

One of the better-looking Light Sixes was this 14 hp Touring Saloon of 1938. The successful 1930s A, B and early D Light Sixes carried a radiator shell which still bore a resemblance to the radiator first seen on the 30-98 and subsequent cars, but from 1937 the 'waterfall' grille took over.

The first completed H-series 10 hp car off the assembly line, 1937. Several Vauxhalls appeared in rallies in the 1930s, including the Ten. T. W. Holtom, beside the car, worked for Vauxhall from 1888 to 1938, and when the motoring journalist Edgar N. Duffield travelled by train to Luton to attend the 1909 Aston Hill Climb, Tommy Holtom met him at the station in the 1908 2000 Miles Trial winner.

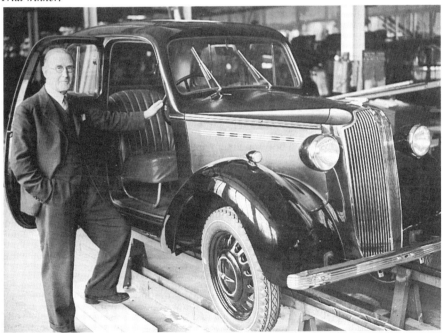

The first new-look postwar Vauxhall was the L-type, 1948. This is the 2.3 litre six-cylinder Velox, little different in appearance from the 1½ litre four-cylinder Wyvern. Gone is the radiator shell and the grille is horizontally barred as on the prewar and postwar I- and J-type radiator shells, whilst bonnet flutes still remain.

Light Sixes for 1937 and 1938 were fitted with a Vauxhall idiosyncrasy, camshaft-driven wipers, which were continued for the next twenty years. These models still had mechanical brakes, but Lockheed hydraulics were fitted to the GY and all subsequent new Vauxhall models from 1938.

The £165 H model Vauxhall 10 was introduced at the 1937 Motor Show, a small three-bearing 1203 cc four-cylinder saloon, the first British car with integral bodywork (no separate chassis), for which the tooling cost £1 million. Three speeds, 6 volt electrics, hydraulic brakes and 65 mph (105 km/h) were offered with 38-42 miles per gallon (6.6-7.3 litres per 100 km). Maurice Olley, suspension expert for Rolls-Royce as well as GM, incorporated torsion bars in the Dubonnet front-suspension units, but there were some problems with the short transverse torsion bars fracturing, as metallurgy was less advanced in those days.

Vauxhall 10s could be available with normal chassis if specialist coachwork was to be fitted. The I-type (for Integral) 12/4 replaced the DY Light Six in 1939 and was an enlarged 10 hp, having a bigger-bore 1442 cc engine and three speeds and 6 volts. The new J-type 14/6 was also integral but still had the original 14 hp 1.8 litre Light Six engine, giving it over 70 mph (112 km/h), but with a new three-speed gearbox with synchromesh on bottom gear as well as on second and top. At £189 and £230 the 12 and 14 hp cars were cheaper than the cars they replaced, lighter due to integral construction and therefore more economical to run. By 1939 the £345 '25' also had three speeds with better acceleration but a lower top speed of 77.59 mph (125 km/h).

During the Second World War Bedford concentrated on vehicles while Vauxhall made all sorts of equipment for the forces, in particular 5460 Churchill tanks, for which they designed a 21 litre flat twelve-cylinder engine.

Initially, with the coming of peace, the 10/4, 12/4 (the last 6 volt Vauxhall) and 14/6 (with optional heater and radio) were resurrected, but with the introduction of the £10 annual flat-rate road tax, regardless of engine size, the 10/4 was dropped from the range.

The first new postwar Vauxhall of 1948 was the L-type, which had the H-type 10 hp body/chassis modified by the Vauxhall stylist David Jones, with new front and rear ends grafted on, a wider grille and an 'alli-

The completely new E-type Wyverns and Veloxes with curved instead of flat windscreens and coil and wishbone independent front suspension appeared at Earl's Court in 1951 but had the L-type engines until spring, 1952, when both were given more powerful 79.4 by 76.2 mm engines. The one-piece bonnet was hinged to open from the front and also from each side, but with limited opening angles.

gator' bonnet opening at the front. There were two versions, the £479 Wyvern (a mythical part-dragon, part-eagle monster, often confused with the griffin) with the familiar 1½ litre 12/4 engine, and the £550 Velox (a 30-98 model name revived) with an increased-bore 14/6 engine giving 2275 cc and better acceleration than that of the 1939 '25' with 76 mph (122.3 km/h). Apart from the engines, the two models differed in their colour schemes; only the Velox had bumper overriders; both had steering-column gear levers and three-speed gear-boxes, but the Velox had no starting handle as the radiator got in the way.

In 1951 completely new Vauxhalls called E-types were introduced, with six-seater, rather bulbous Chevrolet-like bodies and new more powerful short-stroke 'over square' engines by 1952, 1442 cc and 40 bhp in the case of the four-cylinder 75 mph (120.7 km/h) £740 Wyvern, and 2262 cc and 64 bhp in the case of the six-cylinder 80 mph (128.7 km/h) £802 Velox. The Dubonnet front suspension was discarded, as it was unsatisfactory when wear had taken place, and was replaced by coil springs and wishbones. In 1955 the £844 Cresta became the top model and continued to be a Velox with embellishments.

Minor styling changes were made to the E-types from 1954, when the fronts were altered, first with a grille of 'waterfall' chrome strip covering the opening and then in 1956 this horizontal-bar grille with the big V motif, and electric wipers now replaced the mechanically operated ones.

The 2262 cc PA Velox and Cresta six-cylinder models broke with convention with long tailfins and three-piece back windows, though this 1958 Cresta's apparent three-piece curved windscreen is an illusion caused by the sun's reflection. Later 1961-2 PADX/PASY Cresta/Veloxes had one-piece curved rear windows and 2650 cc engines.

TOWARDS HIGH PERFORMANCE WITH OPEL, 1957 ONWARDS

In 1957 the Wyvern was replaced by the £728 55 bhp 1507 cc four-cylinder F-type Victor, memorable for its American looks with wrap-around windscreen, and Detroit also inspired the six-cylinder £983 PA Velox and £1073 Cresta of 2262 cc (82 bhp), which had fins at the rear and increased capacity in 1961 of 2650 cc (95 bhp). A two-speed GM automatic gearbox with fluid flywheel was an alternative on the big cars to the three-speed manual with overdrive. Despite criticisms, the Victor became a best-seller. In 1962 the slightly more expensive FB Victor was noticeably different from the F-type, with sober un-American looks, a 1.6 litre 69 bhp engine from 1964 and an optional floor-change four-speed box. The tuned 90 mph (145 km/h) £971 Victor VX Four Ninety of 1962/3 was the first deliberately sporting Vauxhall since the 30-98, giving 81 bhp by 1964 with front disc brakes as standard. The 1963/4 PB Velox and Cresta models, cost-ing £936 and £1046 respectively, had the sober FB Victor styling enlarged, also with disc brakes, and a 3 litre 113 bhp or a 3.3 litre 128 bhp Chevrolet Six engine of truck origins, the first non-Luton engine fitted to a Vauxhall. This in 140 bhp 3.3 litre form was carried over to the 103 mph (165.7 km/h) PC £1058 Cresta and £1457 Viscount of 1966-72 (Viscount replacing Velox in name but leapfrogging the Cresta in status), with power steering and two-speed Powerglide, then three-speed GM torque converter automatic gearbox or four-speed manual floor change.

The first small Vauxhall since the prewar '10' appeared in 1964, the £528 HA Viva, which was of similarly unprepossessing appearance but had a great future in various forms. Initially it had a 1057 cc pushrod engine with American-style pressed-steel rockers which occasionally broke, four speeds, all synchromesh, and, unusually, transverse-leaf instead of coil-spring in-

The new F-type Victor of 1957 with all coil-spring suspension and wrap-around rear window and windscreen, the forward-sloping pillars of the latter causing some problems with door sealing. Flutes were now relegated to the body sides.

This more conventionally styled 1963 PB Velox Six had an enlarged FB Victor body at a period when the Americans were moving away from 1950s extravagances like tailfins. This Velox had a 2651 cc 113 bhp Chevrolet engine (the first foreign engine in a Vauxhall) and servo-assisted disc front brakes as standard.

The Viva started as a small car, but this is a Mk 1 Viva GT of 1968 with a 2 litre twin-carburettor single ohc slant-four engine tuned by Bill Blydenstein, who reintroduced Vauxhall to racing with this car in 1969-71. The saloon-car racing successes of the big, popular Gerry Marshall made him the most famous Vauxhall racing driver since A. J. Hancock.

dependent front suspension with traditional semi-elliptic springs at the rear, plus rack and pinion steering. By 1965 the 250,000th Viva had been produced and in 1966 production started at the new Vauxhall plant at Ellesmere Port, Cheshire, on the old Hooton Park aerodrome site, once the home of Comper aircraft and Pobjoy aero-engines. In 1968 the impressive Millbrook proving ground was started in Bedfordshire, covering 700 acres (283 hectares). The £579 HB Viva of 1967-70 had an 1159 cc engine, the fashionable 'Coke-bottle' waistline, coil springs and wishbones at the front and a live axle with coil springs replacing leaf springs at the rear.

The 1594 cc FC Victors of 1965-7 were restyled with curved side panels and windows like the Viva, giving thinner doors and more shoulder room, and these and the

This is the FD version of the sporting 2 litre 112 bhp VX 4/90, on sale 1970-2, also with the Viva GT type slant-four engine. The white cross on the grille became associated with the later VX 4/90s though it was not exclusive to them.

The Ventora 11, the last with the 'Coke-bottle' sides, was the upmarket version of the FD Victor and ran from March 1968 to March 1972, with a 140 bhp 3294 cc six-cylinder Chevrolet pushrod engine.

FC VX 4/90s were known as the 101 range. An important car was the FD Victor of 1967-72 with enlarged HB Viva bodywork and the same coil-spring suspension; it was the first production Vauxhall to have a single overhead-camshaft cogged-belt engine, which was slanted at 45 degrees for a low bonnet line, a four-cylinder ('slant four') with five main bearings in 70 bhp 1599 cc and 108 bhp 1975 cc form. Top of the range was the heavier luxury FD Ventora, with the 140 bhp Chevrolet Six engine, and the sporting FD VX 4/90 had the 1975 cc slant four engine tuned to give 112 bhp and 104 mph (167.4 km/h). This engine also powered the rare £1062 Viva GT, livelier than the VX 4/90 as it was lighter, and the HB Viva could also have the 1599 cc slant four engine.

The HC Viva, no longer a 'Coke bottle',

This monster, known as 'Big Bertha', was a special lightened 160 mph (257 km/h) Transcontinental Ventora with a De Dion rear end and an Australian 445 bhp 5 litre Repco-Holden V8 engine raced successfully by Gerry Marshall for six months in 1974 until a brake pad fell out at Silverstone and the car was wrecked. The engine was then put into a Firenza called 'Little Bertha', also raced by Marshall.

A 1974 type FE Victor 2300 SL fitted with radial tyres, which became standard from that year. This was the last Victor, and though its 100 bhp slant four engine was British, the floorpan was German Opel Commodore. The recess in each top corner of the grille and the depressions on the bonnet behind them could almost be seen as a return to the Vauxhall bonnet flutes.

went through a gamut of engines, 1159 cc and 1256 cc pushrod and 1599 cc, 1759 cc (88 bhp) and 2279 cc (110 bhp) slant four. The Viva 1800 and 2300 of 1973 became the upmarket Magnum 1800 and 2300 of 1974-7, the last wholly Luton designs ending in the 1979 1300 and 1800 GLS Vivas as the FE Victors shared a floorpan with the Opel Rekord. The 'Transcontinental' range included the FE Victors (1972-8), the

Ventora Six (1972-6), and 1800 and 2300 models, renamed VX1800 and VX2300 (1976-8), whilst the FE VX 4/90 of 1972-6 had the 110 bhp 2300 engine, increased in 1974-5 to 116 bhp, to reappear in 1977-8 as the VX 490 with 118 bhp and a five-speed German Getrag gearbox.

The Firenza two-door coupé (1971-5) was a sporting HC Viva under a different name using all the Viva engines from 1159

The 'droop-snoot' Firenza two-door sporting coupé of 1971-5 had racing and rally successes from 1972. Vauxhall's reply to Ford's successful Capri was also given a romantic Italian place-name, the Italian for Florence, Firenze, spelt phonetically for easier pronunciation in English.

This is Holman Blackburn's competition Magnum. Magnums scored nine race and rally successes, 1974-7, by drivers such as Pentti Airikkala of Finland, Will Sparrow, Jenny Birrell, Jimmy McRae and Gerry Marshall. The last won his class and came second overall with the Australian Peter Brock in the 1977 Spa 24 Hour Race, the best Vauxhall continental race result since 1913.

cc to 2300 cc. The 1973-5 HP (High Performance) 2300 was given an aerodynamic 'droop-snoot' nose by Dealer Team Vauxhall for competitions, produced 131 bhp and 114 mph (183 km/h) with a five-speed gearbox, and at £2625 cost over twice the price of the basic Firenza. Only 204 were made. The 'droop snoot' was used by other Vauxhalls and copied by other makes.

The HC Viva's successor, the Chevette, at a basic price of £1649 used the Viva 1.3 pushrod engine and Kadett floorpan, 1975-84, and was the first British three-door hatchback, and also a saloon and an estate car. There were two 2300-engined rally versions with Vauxhall-designed sixteen-valve twin-cam heads, the HS of 1976-9 at £5317, giving 135 bhp and 120 mph (193 km/h), and the 1979-80 special production 150 bhp HSR at £7146, of which only fifty were made. The Chevette was a GM 'T' car, a basic design to be built in many countries with suitable modifications under different GM marque names, first marketed in Brazil.

By now design was by Opel, and sales increased rapidly. Opel's Manta and Ascona models bred the 1975 rear-wheel-drive four-cylinder Cavalier, first made in Belgium, then at Luton from 1977, and which was front-wheel-drive by 1981. This was the 'J' car, redesigned from 1988 with

Chevette HSs had eleven rally wins in 1977-9 and Chevette HSRs had the same number in 1980-3, Pentti Airikkala, Jimmy McRae, Tony Pond and Russell Brookes being high scorers. This is Chris Sclater's HS in 1977, entered by Dealer Team Vauxhall and Castrol, as was Airikkala's car.

26

This four-cylinder ohc Carlton was first shown in 1978. Though an Opel Rekord in design, with the biggest of the Opel engines from the Cavalier, it was built at Luton and at least the 'droop-snoot' was British, the Rekord having a barred grille.

front-wheel drive (fwd) or four-wheel drive (4wd), now a justly famous Vauxhall in as many as 35 different versions, including diesel, from 57 to 156 bhp with fuel injection and eight or sixteen valves.

The Carlton (Opel Rekord) of 1978, Luton-built till 1986, supplemented the slightly smaller Cavalier, initially using its biggest engine, replacing the VX, the 2300 GLS version of which, though a four-cylinder, had become top of the range after the Ventora Six was phased out in 1976. Top of the range, 1978-82, was the six-cylinder overhead-camshaft (ohc) Royale, 2.8 or 3 litres, the first Vauxhall with independent rear suspension (irs), though actually an Opel Senator built and Vauxhall-badged in Germany, the coupé version being the Opel Monza. The Opel-built six-cylinder 2.5 litre Viceroy (1980-2) lasted only sixteen months and was an amalgam of Carlton and Royale without the irs. It was succeeded by the Opel Senator (1983), of 2.5 and 3 litres, and the similar Vauxhall Senator (1984-7). These were the 'V' cars; then came the new four- or six-cylinder

A 1980 six-cylinder Royale, a much praised model built at Opel's Russelsheim works, Vauxhall-badged and then sent to England, 1978-82. In 1836 Charles Green went the other way by taking off from Vauxhall Gardens, London, with two passengers in his balloon 'Royal Vauxhall' and landing seventeen hours later at Weilburg, which, like Russelsheim, is near Frankfurt.

The first fwd Vauxhalls were these Astras of 1980 with 1.3 single ohc engines, smaller engines having pushrods with the twin-cam GTE dating from 1988. A GTE won John Cleland the 1989 British Touring Car Championship and Louise Aitken-Walker the 1990 World Ladies' Rally Championship — and an OBE. The engine powers Lotus-approved, Reynard-built single-seaters for British and Opel Euroseries GM Vauxhall-Lotus racing inaugurated in 1988.

Carlton and six-cylinder Senator, (with a slightly longer body than the Carlton on the same wheel-base) from 1986 and 1987 onwards. These have fuel-injected 1.8 (115 bhp), 2.0 (122 bhp) and 2.3 diesel (73 bhp) four-cylinder engines and 2.6 (150 bhp) and 3.0 24-valve (204 bhp) six-cylinder engines. All are rear-wheel drive and German-built.

The first front-wheel-drive Vauxhall, the transverse-engined economy Astra four-cylinder (Opel Kadett, then Opel Astra from 1991), arrived in 1980, British-built at Ellesmere Port from 1981, and took on various forms: hatchback, estate, then booted Belmont from 1985; engines from 1.2 to 2 litres, with a 1.7 litre diesel and the sensational sixteen-valve 'hot hatch' 2 litre

The rare and elegant 2.5 litre Viceroy, 1980-2, was made for only sixteen months in Germany and bears the white cross on its radiator grille, more often associated with VX 4/90s.

The Mk 2 update of the famous Vauxhall Cavalier which gave it transverse-engined front-wheel drive in 1981, after being rear-wheel drive since 1975. Almost a new car from its Mk 3 1988 redesign, the sixteen-valve GSi 2 litre version gained four pole positions and four victories in the 1991 British Touring Car Racing Championship, in which John Cleland came second to a BMW.

135 mph (217 km/h) GTE from 1988, becoming the more spacious GSi from 1991, still with 150 bhp. Astras were updated in 1984 and 1991.

The small four-cylinder fwd Nova (Opel Corsa), launched in 1983, was the GM 'S'

car, built in the GM Spanish plant using 1 to 1.8 litre engines, including a refined and responsive 1.7 Isuzu turbo diesel model from 1991 (Isuzu being the GM Japanese arm). The 1988 117 mph (188 km/h) 100 bhp GTE was renamed the 1.6 GSi in late

The British Racing and Sports Car Club's Thundersaloons racing category is descended from the Special Saloons of the 1970s featuring the 'Bertha' V8s. This is the John Cleland/Vince Woodman Chevrolet-engined V8 Carlton which won the Class A main category in 1988 and 1989. Pete Stevens and Chris Millard were the 1990 winners with a Senator V8 and they were second in a 6 litre Carlton V8 in 1991.

A 1991 fwd Nova Spin 993 cc pushrod hatchback made at General Motors' Zaragoza plant in Spain. Novas date originally from 1983 and ohc ones had class wins in rallies from 1984. From 1990 Vauxhall Dealer Sport instituted the 1.6 GSi Nova Rallycross Challenge saloon racing series, whilst new talent was developed by Formula Vauxhall Junior racing from 1991 using Van Diemen wingless single-seaters with 112 bhp Nova GSi engines on leadless fuel.

1990 when Novas were given a more rounded look.

Remarkable 1990s Vauxhalls are the Cavalier-based Astra-engined front- or four-wheel-drive 2 litre eight- or sixteen-valve 115 or 150 bhp Calibra (201 bhp in four-wheel-drive sixteen-valve turbo form), at launch the most aerodynamic coupé in the world, styled by GM's Wayne Cherry, initially made in Germany, then in the GM Saab plant in Finland (Saab being 50 per cent GM owned), and the British-built lim-ited-production £48,000 rear-drive six-speed Vauxhall Lotus Carlton, at launch the fastest saloon in the world at 176 mph (283 km/h) with a notably economical 24-valve twin-cam, twin-turbo, 3.6 litre six-cylinder 382 bhp engine. GM acquired Lotus at the end of 1985.

From the IBC Vehicles Limited former Bedford van factory at Luton have come the Japanese Isuzu-designed, British-built Vauxhall Frontera off-road cars with five-speed rear-wheel drive for road use and

A 1992 140 mph (225 km/h) Senator CD with a six-cylinder 3 litre 24-valve engine, also used in the Carlton offering ABS anti-lock braking, catalytic converter, selectable firmness suspension and so on. An automatic gearbox is standard, with five-speed manual as a no-cost option.

This 1991/2 sixteen-valve 2 litre four-wheel-drive version Calibra coupé, styled by Wayne Cherry, epitomises the low-drag policy on modern Vauxhalls, helping fuel economy. The drag factor is slightly better on the 115 mph (185 km/h) eight-valve Calibra as it has a smaller radiator air intake compared with the 139 mph (224 km/h) sixteen-valve version.

selectable two-speed transfer four-wheel drive for off roads, in short-chassis Sport and long-chassis Estate form, the former with a 2 litre Cavalier petrol engine and the latter with 2.4 litre petrol or 2.3 turbo diesel Opel engines, both models competitively priced in a popular market. From the same stable has come since 1990 the Vauxhall Albany all-purpose 'people carrier' with seven comfortable seats, two sunroofs, pile carpet and a stereo system, and, as it is based on the 1985 one-ton Midi van with 2 litre Isuzu engine, it is roomy and not expensive in its field.

Long- and short-chassis Fronteras from the former Bedford van IBC Vehicles factory at Luton, the big Bedford truck plant at Dunstable having been sold to AWD Limited after production ceased in 1986. The Bedford badge was suddenly dropped in the summer of 1990, being replaced by the Vauxhall name on Opel-designed Astra vans from Ellesmere Port and Isuzu-designed Fronteras and Midi vans, and for Suzuki-designed Rascal vans from IBC.

FURTHER READING

Alder, Trevor. *Vauxhall — The Postwar Years*. Haynes-Foulis, 1991.
Derbyshire, L. C. *The Story of Vauxhall, 1857-1946*. Vauxhall Motors, 1947.
Platt, Maurice. *An Addiction to Automobiles*. Frederick Warne, 1980.
Ruppert, James. *Vauxhall Driver's Book*. Haynes-Foulis, 1990.
Sedgwick, Michael. *Vauxhall — A Pictorial Tribute*. Beaulieu Books, 1981.
Stanford, John. *The 30-98 Vauxhall*. Profile Publication number 32, 1966.
The Griffin Story. Vauxhall Motors, 1990.
A History of Vauxhall. Vauxhall Motors, 1980.

CLUBS

F Vauxhall Victor Owners' Club: Old Station, Eastville, Boston, Lincolnshire PE22 8LS.
Opel-Vauxhall Drivers' Club: 32A High Street, Dereham, Norfolk NR19 1DR. Telephone: 0362 694459.
Royale Monza Owners' Club: Sheila Godden, 2 Caxton Court, Roman Road, Luton, Bedfordshire LU3 2QS.
Vauxhall Droop-Snoot Group: 28 Second Avenue, Ravenswing Park, Aldermaston, Berkshire RG7 4PX. Telephone: 0734 815238.
Vauxhall Owners' Club: Ron Shier, 41 Oxleys Cottages, Haynes West End, Bedford MK45 3QT. For all Vauxhalls from 1903 to the last of the E series in 1957.
Vauxhall PA, PB, PC and E Owners' Club: Steve Chapman, 338 Eastcote Lane, South Harrow, Middlesex HA2 8RY.
Vauxhall 30-98 Register: David Marsh, The Garden House, Middleton by Youlgreave, Bakewell, Derbyshire DE4 1LS.
Vauxhall Victor 101 Club: Mrs L. Pearce, 12 Cliff Crescent, Ellerdine, Telford, Shropshire.
Vauxhall Viva Owners' Club: Adrian Miller, The Thatches, Snetterton, Norwich NR16 2LD. Telephone: 095382 8818.
Vauxhall VX 4/90 Owners' Club: Mike Nash, 43 Stroudwater Park, St George's Avenue, Weybridge, Surrey KT13 0DT.

PLACES TO VISIT

Museum displays may be altered and readers are advised to telephone before visiting to check that the Vauxhalls are on show, as well as to find out the opening times.

Haynes Sparkford Motor Museum, Sparkford, near Yeovil, Somerset BA22 7LH. Telephone: 0963 40804. 1960 Cresta PA, 1961 Victor de Luxe and others.
National Motor Museum, John Montagu Building, Beaulieu, Brockenhurst, Hampshire SO42 7ZN. Telephone: 0590 612345. 1915 Prince Henry, 1938 10 hp.
The Patrick Collection, 180 Lifford Lane, King's Norton, Birmingham, West Midlands B30 3NT. Telephone: 021-459 9111. Vauxhalls 1960 to 1990, Cresta, Victor, Chevette, et cetera.
Science Museum, Exhibition Road, South Kensington, London SW7 2DD. Telephone: 071-938 8000. 1903 5 hp single-cylinder.